MW00639728

REMOTE 101

The Secret to Engaging Virtual Workers

REMOTE 101

101

The Secret to Engaging
Virtual Workers

JILL CHRISTENSEN

Remote 101
by Jill Christensen

Copyright © 2022 Jill Christensen

Published by
Knightsbridge Press

ISBN: 978-0-9974764-1-5
Library of Congress Cataloging-in-Publication Data

Christensen, Jill
Remote 101
The Secret to Engaging Virtual Workers

Printed and bound in the United States of America

THE GUTS

GRATITUDE

To my parents. I appreciate you setting the bar high and giving me the self-confidence to leap. Thanks to you, I'm pursuing my dreams and following my purpose with reckless abandon.

IMPORTANT NOTES

This book was written for managers, so they can engage their remote team members. Additionally, many of the ideas can be used to engage and inspire employees who are not remote, if you are working in a hybrid environment. It can also be used by business owners, senior leaders, business unit or department heads, or Human Resources (HR) professionals to engage virtual workers in an entire organization.

The simple, straight-forward solutions I present work for a five-person team or a 250,000-person organization. Why? Because all employees are human beings, and all human beings are wired similarly.

Want more critical insights that will overhaul the way you think and make you work life substantially easier? Just turn the page.

CHAPTER 1

The Future of Work

"One day, offices will be a thing of the past."

– Sir Richard Branson is an English business magnate, investor, and author. Branson founded the Virgin Group, which controls more than 400 companies in various fields.

March 11, 2020. It was exactly six months to the day before the 19th anniversary of 9/11 and a day that – like 9/11 – will go down in infamy. This time, however, the culprit was not the Islamic extremist group Al-Qaeda, who coordinated a series of four terrorist attacks against the United States. This time, the culprit was COVID-19.

A variant of the flu, which experts believe originated in China, COVID-19 quickly began its global reign of terror. No one was completely safe. Few were immune. Like 9/11, once again the world was under attack, and the familiar patterns of life and work changed monumentally, perhaps forever.

The World Health Organization (WHO) declared COVID-19 a global pandemic on March 11, 2020. Companies across the world closed their workplaces and told employees to work from home. Social distancing became the new buzz phrase and masks an essential new wardrobe must-have item.

COVID-19
[ko-vid-nine-teen]
Noun
1. respiratory illness caused by a coronavirus, transmitted chiefly by contact with infectious material, or contaminated objects or surfaces.

At that time, we thought we'd be fighting the siege for weeks, possibly months. And then reality set in. Little did we know that a massive, long-term social experiment was about to begin.

The Reality

Hundreds of millions of workers stranded at home, disconnected from their co-workers and organizations, working remotely. Flying solo. Managers were separated from their teams, who they could no longer physically see or come in contact with. This left many managers to fret over these burning questions, with no clear answers:

- "What are my people doing all day?"
- "Are my employees OK?"
- "How do I know people are working if I can't physically see them?"
- "Have my people checked out?"
- "How the heck do I inspire people via Zoom?"
- "Can people really focus and be productive working remotely?"
- "Are my employees still engaged?"
- "How is this separation going to negatively impact our results?"

- "How am I going to lead people from afar?"
- "When is this going to be over?"

Suffice it to say, most employers would not have chosen this social experiment; it was forced upon them. We've had to innovate, and become more nimble, flexible, resilient, kind, and open-minded.

But Open-Minded Typically Isn't Our Strength

When I worked in global Internal Communications in Corporate America for two decades, I would regularly approach HR about the need for our company to have a telecommuting policy. Why? Because employees were clamoring for it.

The vast majority of the time, the answer was, "No," because senior leaders did not trust that employees would be productive at home. Leaders wanted to physically see employees working – in the flesh.

open-minded
[o-pen-myne-ded]
Adjective
1. receptive to new and different ideas or the opinions of others.

When managers and leaders can physically see employees working, they think they are being productive. Some even think that because an employee gets out of bed, showers, and shows up in a physical office setting, that they are engaged and want to be there. However, this is a fallacy. Many employees are simply 'going through the motions,' unbeknownst to managers and leaders.

Lessons Learned

The COVID-19 crisis taught us a lot.

We meet too much. You can wear pajama bottoms or sweatpants on a Zoom call because people can only see you from the waist up. Employees in an office setting are not more productive than remote workers ("Remoties"). Dropbox and shared file systems that connect to the cloud are indispensable and priceless. The sense of connection we feel to co-workers and to the organization gets lost when we are not physically co-located. As managers, we must do things differently to ensure people stay engaged.

Some companies plan to remain 100 percent remote post-pandemic, while others will choose a hybrid model where employees will have choices about where and when they work. Others will demand that everyone come back.

Whatever option your organization chooses, I think this forced experiment will ultimately be proven good for both employers and employees alike. Leaders now see that telecommuting does work and many employees will now have options not afforded to them pre-pandemic.

COVID-19 pressed the fast-forward button and we learned about the immediate, practical future of work, in a hurry. In a nutshell? Work as we know it has changed – forever. And many times in life, when a major change occurs, it means we must re-invent ourselves not only in order to survive, but to thrive.

> **thrive**
> [th-rye-hv]
> *Verb*
> 1. to prosper; be fortunate or successful.
> 2. to grow or develop vigorously; flourish.

For those of you who know me, have read my first book (*If Not You, Who? Cracking the Code of Employee Disengagement*), or heard me speak, you know that I think surviving is not the name of the game. Surviving is the basement. Thriving is the penthouse. As business leaders, the penthouse is where I want all of you – and your organizations – to be.

Why Does All of This Matter?

There are two reasons why knowing how to engage Remoties is such an important topic.

1. First, according to Salesforce, an American cloud-based software company, 61 percent of workers are now working from home fulltime. Yet only 49 percent of those remote workers agree that their organization cares about their overall well-being. Needless to say, this is a recipe for disaster and employee disengagement.

2. Second, engaging remote workers is an important topic because effective employee engagement reaps enormous benefits. Reams of data shows that engaged workers are more productive, provide better customer service, make fewer mistakes, stay longer, are more creative, are passionate brand ambassadors, are absent less, steal less, produce a better-quality product, and recommend their company as a great place to work to their family and friends. And what do all of these benefits lead to? Increased revenue growth, greater profits, and outperforming your competitors.

The equation looks like this: When YOU put employees first, THEY will give you their all, engage, and put customers first. When customers are put first, their experience is exemplary

– better than what your competitors offer – so, they keep coming back to your organization for more. The result? Increased revenue growth, a more attractive bottom line, and the satisfaction that comes from knowing you are the best in your industry.

revenue growth
[rev-en-you gro-th]
Noun
1. income or sales increases over time; used to measure how fast a business is expanding.

At the end of the day, your organization's strength, and its future success, lies in your workers. Historically, companies depended on their high performers at headquarters to pull the vast majority of the weight. Now that employees are dispersed, it is even more important that everyone contributes equally. And trust me when I say that the best way to achieve this is to have team members who are highly engaged, running on all cylinders.

Pillow Talk About Tomorrow

Now that we have defined what we are experiencing today, let's talk about tomorrow – or the future of work – because in my opinion, savvy leaders do three things: they learn from the past, they live in the present, and they imagine the future.

According to Alex Sixt, an *Entrepreneur NEXT* expert, "Before COVID-19 spread globally, a transformation had already begun to steer businesses toward a digital approach. The pandemic greatly accelerated this change, forcing businesses to find efficient ways to connect outside of the office, and most of these changes are here to stay."

pillow talk
[pill-oh tawk]
Noun
1. an easy conversation in a safe and comfortable space.

Here are four significant trends that Sixt advises managers to keep an eye on:

1. **Going remote.**
   Remote working is the norm for many businesses, and it will likely stay because leaders have learned that employees can perform just as well outside of a physical office building as they can in one. According to Owl Labs, a company that makes 360° video conferencing devices, 83 percent of employees say that a remote work opportunity would make them feel happier at their job.

And although the over-arching goal is not happiness – it is engagement – (we'll get to that in Chapter 2) employee happiness increases productivity. Research by Oxford University's Said Business School, in collaboration with British multinational telecommunications holding company BT, found that workers are 13 percent more productive when they are happy in their work environment.

JPMorgan Chase agrees. According to Jamie Dimon, chairman and CEO, the future workplace will be most successful if employees go to an office at least part-time, as it enables them to know one another, learn from mentors, increase the speed at which decisions are made, and build synergy from live interaction.

2. **The digital transformation.**
The role that technology plays in the way we work will become even more important in the future. The digital transformation is not about replacing employees with technology, but rather digitalizing the processes used in business.

The current digital transformation is centered around solving problems for teams, using technologies that connect to the cloud, such as Microsoft Teams, Slack, and Google Drive. The 'old ways' of how employees work are not efficient and effective, and they do not support an enhanced telecommuting experience.

3. **Millennial takeover.**
Millennials are tech-savvy and open to working in new ways. As the 'Boomer' generation begins to phase out of the workforce, Millennials are beginning to fill the leadership positions of older executives. This passing of the torch means our new leaders will value innovation, learning, and quick adaption and deployment, vs. process perfection.

Another value Millennials hold closely? The ability to work remotely and have a flexible schedule. Technology has made work accessible anywhere, anytime, so Millennials can work hours that are convenient for them and achieve better work-life balance. As Millennials take over the workforce, these values will define the future of work.

4. **The need for a scalable workforce.**
As the business landscape changes, the size of a business' workforce will need to adjust as well. A scalable staff enables an organization to be flexible and adjust as needed. Hiring full-time employees is expensive and the process can be lengthy. In our rapidly changing world, a flexible workforce is a reality which organizations must be open to exploring.

Fortunately, there are a variety of companies that offer flexible talent solutions on-demand, such as Upwork and Fiverr. These companies enable you to engage people worldwide to meet your short-term or recurring talent needs, which will help you succeed in the future of work.

Desired Remotie Qualities

Regardless of whether you hire full-time employees or engage short-term gig workers, the future of work will be defined by organizations having a mix of both on-site and remote employees. This is the hybrid model.

Therefore, let's look at essential traits for a great remote worker.

> **trait**
> [trayt]
> *Noun*
> 1. a distinguishing quality (as of personal character).

Mike Swigunski, a contributing writer for the Entrepreneur Leadership Network, founder of Globalcareer.io, and author of the *Global Career Book*, says, "It can be tricky to find the right remote employee who can deliver the work you expect."

According to Swigunski, there are four essential traits found in the best remote workers. As you seek to build a team of passionate, effective, engaged, and inspired remote workers, these traits are character qualities you should consider seeking out.

- **Self-motivated.** An effective remote worker can operate independently and be productive without constant check-ins with their manager. Somebody who is not able to motivate themselves or prioritize work in order to meet deadlines, will not thrive as a remote worker. A stellar remote employee will ask for project logistics and deadlines before they begin working.

  Unfortunately, it can be difficult to determine if someone is self-motivated just by reviewing their resume or CV. Therefore, craft interview questions to determine what motivates the applicant and ask for real-life examples of self-motivation. Laziness and procrastination do not bode well for remote workers.

- **Tech-savvy.** If you hire the right remote workers, they will be able to easily navigate common online portals. You cannot thrive as a remote worker unless you are tech-savvy, and comfortable with computers and the latest technology.

This trait is normally pretty easy to find in a remote worker. However, it is a great filtering tactic to ask for a technical task in an interview. It can be as simple as requesting the applicant to create and send a short introduction video through an online platform.

- **Skilled communicator.** Communication is the most essential trait of remote workers. Remote workers who are poor communicators will struggle to thrive in a virtual environment. This is why you should check for communication skills while interviewing potential remote employees.

  During an interview, it is normally very easy to tell if somebody is a skilled communicator. If there are doubts, utilize a communication aptitude test. Skilled communication includes being direct, clear, professional, and asking for specific help when they are unsure of how to proceed with work.

- **Collaborative.** The ability to work together as a team is something that can be taught, as most people don't inherently possess this skill. As an employer, you can help employees by creating a climate for collaboration. The key is to make expectations clear when discussing new projects, while simultaneously enabling your workers to have freedom to put their own ideas and authenticity to work.

Remote workers cannot deliver results in the absence of guidance. Instead, outline the guidelines, leave room for improvement, and give people a runway to soar.

Time to Dive In

Now that we have a picture of the current landscape, what the future of work holds, and the type of people who are best suited to work in a remote environment, let us dive into employee engagement.

> **dive**
> [dyevuh]
> *Verb*
> 1. to plunge head-first.

Although you may have employees who possess the four essential traits that are found in the best Remoties, if these people are disengaged, they will not go above and beyond the call of duty and give you a lot of discretionary effort.

Will they shower and show-up every day? Yes, but they will be giving you scraps – doing what they have to do to get by – and that will not enable your customers or your organization to soar. It will also make your life as a manager suck. The truth will set you free.

CHAPTER 2

What Exactly is Employee Engagement, Anyway?

"Everyone talks about building a relationship with your customer. I think you build one with your employees first."

– **Angela Ahrendts** is an American businesswoman who was previously the senior vice president of retail at Apple. She was ranked 25th in *Forbes*' list of the most powerful women in the world, 9th most powerful woman in the U.K.

One of the most important takeaways from this book is the definition of employee engagement. Engaged employees trust their leaders (managers are leaders) and feel an emotional connection to the organization. And because of this, they go above and beyond the call of duty, and give you a lot of additional discretionary effort.

> **discretionary**
> [dis-kresh-en-air-ee]
> *Adjective*
> 1. subject or left to one's own discretion.

This is why employee engagement matters. Your employees show up for work every day and they have a choice: They can do the ordinary, or the extraordinary. They can show initiative and go above and beyond, or give you scraps. And I am not just talking about the time they spend engaged, but the quality of that time. How an employee is treated – and the culture in which they are being asked to do their job – has a major bearing on the choice they make.

Bottom-line, if an employee's needs and expectations are met at work (we will discuss their needs in detail in Chapter 6), there is an excellent chance they will engage and go above and beyond the call of duty. If their needs are not met, the odds increase greatly that they will check out and do what they have to do to get by.

Categories of Worker Engagement

- **Engaged:** Employees feel a strong emotional connection to the organization. They drive innovation, trust, move the company forward, are loyal, and more enthusiastically follow their leaders.

- **Disengaged:** Employees sleepwalk through their day, putting time – but no creativity, energy, or passion – into their work. They run on a hamster wheel and do what they have to do to get by.

- **Actively Disengaged:** Employees do not just sleepwalk through their day; they act out on their lack of engagement. These workers spread gossip and rumors, engage in toxic office politics, and purposely sabotage their co-worker's efforts and accomplishments.

employee engagement
[em-ploi-ee in-gage-ment]
Noun
1. an employee who trusts their leader and has an emotional connection to the organization.

Happy is Not Engaged

Many employee engagement and leadership experts say that the goal is to build a happy workforce, but I disagree. As you already know, engaged employees trust leaders and feel an emotional connection to the organization. And because you have captured their head and their heart, they go above and beyond the bare minimum, and give you a lot of positive, productive discretionary effort.

Happy employees are, well, happy. They are cheerful, merry, and blissful. This does not mean they will go the extra mile. Period. In fact, one reason they might be happy is because they do not work very hard, but still collect a large paycheck.

happy
[hap-ee]
Adjective
1. a feeling of joy, delight, or glee.

A few years ago, office dogs, ping-pong tables, and kegerators filled with free beer were all the rage in workplaces. I am convinced that organizations purchased these items because they thought, or hoped, they would increase employee camaraderie, morale, teamwork, and engagement.

Do these perks cause people to be happier? Absolutely. Who wouldn't smile if a Golden Retriever puppy were slobbering on them in a meeting, while they were drinking a frosty, cold microbrew? But happy is not engaged.

A study by the U.S. Chamber of Commerce Foundation found that 53 percent of employees say that employee perks give them a better quality of life, which is wonderful news. I'm all for a better quality of life. But the mistake many organizations make is they think office dogs, ping-pong tables, and kegerators double as an employee engagement strategy. And this simply is not true. You need both.

You need office perks, and you need a strategy to engage or re-engage employees. Fido, or sleeping pods, of and by themselves are not going to cut it. The organizations that turn their culture around have embarked on an employee engagement journey, where they discover what is wrong, make changes, measure their progress, communicate the progress with employees, and course-correct if necessary. In order to succeed at culture change, you must approach it strategically.

Employee Engagement is Not Difficult

Now you may be thinking, "An employee engagement strategy? That sounds grueling and time consuming." People whine at me all the time (yes, when someone frowns and rolls their eyes, it's whining), "Employee engagement is so difficult." The truth? It is not difficult.

The definition of culture is: How we do things here. Every company has one – positive, neutral, or negative – whether it is aware of it or not. If you exist, you have one. And in order for you to change your culture and re-engage employees, you simply need to do things here differently tomorrow than you are doing them today. It's that straight-forward. We will discuss exactly what managers should do differently in Chapters 7-10, as it is based on what employees say they need.

culture
[kul-chur]
Noun
1. how we do things here.

The keys to an extraordinary company culture are awareness and consistency. When every manager gets onboard and executes consistently in the areas that are proven to drive employee engagement, your organization's culture will improve.

And if an organization is not interested in embarking on a culture journey, then a manager can simply own, direct, and be accountable for the culture they create on their individual team.

The operative words here are 'execute consistently.' Currently, in most organizations, Manager A is a great leader, so their employees are engaged. Manager B is a mediocre leader, so some of their employees are engaged and others are disengaged. Manager C is a crappy leader, so their employees are actively disengaged.

bipolar
[by-poe-ler]
Adjective
1. having or relating to two poles or extremities.

This is why most organizations have what I call a 'bipolar culture.' The entire organization is not dysfunctional. There are pockets of strong leaders with engaged teams, but it is not the norm in the organization because managers are not executing consistently. They are doing whatever the heck they want because no one is holding them accountable for being a great people leader and many have not been trained.

Managers: Thrown to the Wolves

Managers are not completely to blame for the rampant levels of global employee disengagement. A study by Career-Builder.com shows that a whopping 58 percent of managers said they did not receive any management training. And 87 percent of middle managers wish they had received more management training when they first became a supervisor. We have a lot of leaders who are not trained on how to lead.

Most people in the workforce get promoted into management because they are excellent at their current job. Few people are promoted because they are excellent leaders of people. So, it's not surprising that employee engagement is a global epidemic, because most managers have not been taught how to lead – let alone, engage remote workers. Until now.

Before we dive into the solution, let's look at the benefits of having engaged employees, as they are immense.

grasshopper
[gras-ha-per]
Noun
1. plant-eating orthopteras insects having hind legs adapted for leaping.
2. a student/disciple.

It should be music to your ears to learn that when you build a team of engaged employees, your life as a manager will be easier. And not a little easier; a lot easier. My goal is to help you do that, so you never have misgivings about leading people again. I get it – I have walked a mile in your shoes. Additionally, building a team of engaged employees is usually a nice career-builder, as you are successfully spawning change.

Onward and upward, young grasshopper.

CHAPTER 3

How Engaged Employees Drive Results & Make Life Easier

"The achievements of an organization are the results of the combined effort of each individual."

– Vince Lombardi was an American football coach and executive in the National Football League (NFL). He led the Green Bay Packers to five championships in seven years and won the first two Super Bowls.

Amazon. The Brazilian soccer team. Salesforce. The Virgin Group. The New England Patriots football team. Apple. The Ritz-Carlton Hotel Company. What do these organizations have in common? They win.

And why do they win? They win because they have employees who trust leaders, who feel an emotional connection to the organization, and who will stop at nothing to ensure the people they serve – customers and/or fans – are delighted.

In short, these organizations win because their employees are engaged.

When you have an amazing culture and employees are engaged, performance skyrockets and everyone benefits: customers, management, the board of directors, shareholders, and every other entity that interacts with your business.

success
[suck-sess]
Noun
1. a favorable or desirable outcome.

Engagement Drives Dollars

In addition, company success is assured. According to Gallup, organizations with the highest levels of employee engagement outperform their peers by 147 percent in earnings per share, and have a 90 percent better growth trend than their competition. It is an undeniable truth that there is a direct correlation between employee engagement and profitability.

The most profitable companies in the world, which are growing the fastest, have some of the highest levels of employee engagement. They also realize other important benefits, including:

- Increased employee productivity and retention.

- Increased ability to cherry-pick high performers away from your competitors.

- Increased employee loyalty, pride, and creativity.

- Increased customer service and customer satisfaction.

- Increased satisfaction knowing that you are 'tops' in your industry.

- Decreased safety incidents and theft.

- Decreased training costs, thanks to lower turnover.

- Decreased employee absenteeism and employee turnover.

- Decreased quality defects and mistakes.

Employees who trust their leaders and who feel emotionally connected to the organization go the extra mile. They do everything they can to ensure the company succeeds, with no pushing or prodding. They freely and proudly give you outstanding discretionary effort – their blood, sweat, and tears – every day, which pays enormous dividends.

When you create an environment that people love, they will give you the shirts off their backs, provide an extraordinary customer experience, and your customers will come back for more. And that's how profits soar.

> **sweat**
> [s-whet]
> *Verb*
> 1. to labor or exert oneself.

With this reality in mind, it stands to reason that re-engaging employees who have 'checked out,' is one of the simplest ways to improve organizational productivity, performance, and profitability. Your team and your organization will never soar if you do not step-up and awaken this untapped potential.

You Always Wanted to be a Psychologist, Right?

As mentioned earlier, a study by CareerBuilder.com shows that 58 percent of managers said they didn't receive any management training, which means the majority of leaders were never taught how to engage their employees.

And even if you have received managerial training, it's no secret that being a people leader is not a simple task. I have managed a lot of people and from my experience, if you manage others, you spend a lot of your time acting as a psychologist. This takes precious time away from you getting your own work done and, even worse, it is mentally exhausting.

> **psychologist**
> [sy-kol-o-gist]
> *Noun*
> 1. a person who studies normal and abnormal mental states, perceptual, cognitive, emotional, and processes behavior.

However, when you build a team of engaged employees, your job will become easier. Much easier. Engaged employees tend to be more independent, proactive, courageous, creative, satisfied, and self-confident. They are self-starters.

All of this is code for: these employees create fewer problems and have fewer issues that you have to deal with.

Now that all of this compelling data has been presented to you, I'm confident you are starting to see the light. Because let's face it ... if you have disengaged employees on your team – people who show up each day and do the bare minimum – this will absolutely impact you and not in a good way. People who do what they have to do to get by, or who have a crappy negative attitude, are toxic to your team. And they cause you an abundant amount of stress and problems, things you do not need.

In general, disengaged employees bring to the table performance issues that you have to deal with. They bring other people on your team down, they miss goals and milestones, they start office gossip and rumors, they are absent more, they provide mediocre customer service, they steal more, and they make more mistakes. And if you have not figured it out, that makes you look bad because your employee's morale, culture, and performance are a reflection of leadership – yours.

You might be thinking this environment sounds like crap. Yes, is it crap, and something you can avoid by building an engaged team. A team who trusts you, runs on all cylinders, goes above and beyond the call of duty, and gives you 110 percent discretionary effort every day.

The Role of the Manager

What is your role as a manager as it relates to employee engagement? In one word: Everything. I know that's probably not what you want to hear, especially at a time when there are so many new obstacles on the table. Expectations have never been higher for managers, as we all come to grips with the fact that our new world of remote work is here to stay in some form.

Today, great managers must be skilled at people management, leadership, communication, collaboration, critical thinking, managing up, project management, new technology, time management, prioritization, coaching, delegation, and problem solving. And, you must also support your team, by giving people the motivation, inspiration, and tools to succeed.

Oh, and then there's your 'day job' that you are responsible for accomplishing. And now we can add remote worker engagement to the list.

Why does employee engagement fall squarely on the shoulders of managers? Because you are a key conduit to helping employees feel connected, inspired, and involved.

You know the saying: People leave managers, not companies. It's true. According to a Gallup poll, 50 percent of employees who quit their job cite their manager as the reason.

> **people manager**
> [pee-pol ma-na-jer]
> *Noun*
> 1. a person who directs a team.

The manager/employee relationship is highly correlated with employee engagement. For this reason, it is your responsibility to upskill yourself, so you have the information, tools, resources, and inspiration to lead effectively, and build an engaged team. In order for employee engagement to soar on a team or in an organization, managers must take accountability for it, prioritize it, strategize how to do it, measure progress, and change course if the desired results are not being achieved.

The truth? Everything in business rises and falls as a result of leadership. If a company has high levels of employee engagement and meets or exceeds its goals, odds are, managers are owning up to their responsibilities and executing.

When you create an environment that people love, where they can soar, you will see a measurable change in your workforce. Employees will become more self-confident, courageous, optimistic, passionate, productive, and creative. Consequently, your business performance and profitability will increase.

You: An Extension of the Senior Leadership Team

Many managers do not think of themselves this way, but in reality, you are an extension of the senior leadership team. You have graduated from being an individual performer into being a leader.

As the title of my first book asks, *If Not You, Who?* You chose to be a leader – a dealer in hope. With that choice, you signed up for a huge responsibility: To ensure your organization and your people succeed.

hope
[ho-puh]
Verb
1. desire accompanied by belief in fulfillment.

The quickest path to that goal is to re-engage your most valuable asset: the employees on your team. Engaged employees give you their blood, sweat, and tears. Disengaged employees give you scraps. It is the truth. For this reason, disengaged employees offer the greatest untapped potential for you to improve productivity, performance, profitability, and your personal state of mind.

How important is this? You would be wise to remember that there is one of you, and many of them. No matter how good you are at accomplishing your own tasks and challenges, your teams' overall achievements and success will be elevated if more team members are engaged. It's simple math.

This being the case, one would think that organizations and managers are making employee engagement a priority and hitting the ball out of the park. Unfortunately, that's wrong. The vast majority of organizations – in every country, in every industry, at every size – are failing. Although I'm an optimist, I also pride myself in facing reality. So how bad it is? It's dismal.

CHAPTER 4

The Dismal State of Engagement Worldwide

"So much of what we call management consists of making it difficult for people to work."

– **Peter Drucker** was an Austrian management consultant, educator, and author, whose writings contributed to the practical foundations of the modern business corporation.

You just read powerful data in Chapter 3 about the benefits of having engaged workers, and how it will make your life as a manager easier. However, the vast majority of organizations – in every country, in every industry, at every size – are getting a failing grade. Some are trying, but in most instances, their efforts are falling short.

Gallup, Inc., an American analytics and advisory company based in Washington, D.C., has been continuously tracking workforce engagement and well-being since 2009.

well-being
[wel-bee-ing]
Noun
1. the state of being happy, healthy, or prosperous.

Although the statistics on employee engagement are a moving target and the numbers change frequently, the Gallup State of the Global Workplace 2021 Report contains the following data. (To download the full report and see engagement numbers by region and country, visit *https://www.gallup.com.*)

- 20 percent of global employees are engaged at work.

- 36 percent of U.S. employees are engaged at work.

- Best-practice organizations average 73 percent employee engagement.

This shows that 80 percent of all worldwide workers are disengaged. Not exactly a recipe for business success.

According to the *Gallup Business Journal*, 70 percent of the variance in engagement is explained by the quality of the manager. Teams with engaged managers are more likely to be engaged, are more resilient, and record higher levels of employee well-being.

While it's a positive sign to note that employees who work remotely at least some of the time have the highest levels of engagement, the numbers are still downright dismal.

Did You Dream of Getting F's as a Child?

If you scored 20 percent positive on a test, you would receive an 'F'. Clearly, we can – and should – do better. And as a manager, you are at the heart of making this happen.

> **F**
> [ef]
> *Noun*
> 1. a grade that is not high enough to pass an examination or test.
> 2. a failing grade.

As reported by Gallup, managers affect 70 percent of the variance in team engagement. Kristin Ryba, a brand strategist at Quantum Workplace, puts it this way, "Employees naturally gauge their connection and engagement with an organization through their local relationships and environments. And no one has a greater influence on those day-to-day interactions, processes, and operations than the managers who are on the ground with them."

Ryba goes on to say that the most effective managers build personalized relationships and connections with their employees. Then they leverage individual strengths to empower and inspire their people and the team, which drives engagement.

Are You Serious?

As a former manager, I know what you may be thinking: "You seriously cannot think that I have time for this – I don't." While I understand this reaction, because time is the most precious thing we have, please hear me out.

In Chapter 3, we established that the manager/employee relationship is highly correlated with employee engagement. Trust me when I say that you do not want disengaged workers on your team. Your life as a manager will be miserable. Disengaged employees suck your passion, suck your energy, suck your time, suck your results, and suck your spirit.

suck
[suh-k]
Verb
1. to pull with great force.
2. your life if you have disengaged employees on your team.

The absolute best use of your time is to build a team of highly engaged employees. When employees are engaged, they are more independent, rely on you less, and take up less of your valuable time. Let me repeat that. When employees are engaged, they are more independent, rely on you less, and take up less of your valuable time. This enables you to have more time to focus on your 'day job,' because you will spend less time dealing with problems and playing the role of psychologist.

Some organizations understand that employee engagement should be a top priority for managers, so they provide them with the tools, resources, strategies, and support to succeed. Other organizations simply don't get it. However, even among the organizations that do get it, many still do not succeed. So, the big question on the table is, "Why?"

CHAPTER 5

Why Organizations Fail at Engagement

"Do not judge me by my successes, judge me by how many times I fell down and got back up again."

– Nelson Mandela was a South African anti-apartheid revolutionary, political leader, and philanthropist, who served as President of South Africa from 1994 to 1999.

One of the most interesting things about employee disengagement is that it doesn't happen overnight. Each of your employees showed up for their first day at work 100 percent engaged.

New employees are willing to give you everything they have. They get excited about going above and beyond the call of duty. They have visions of being rated a high performer. They dream about succeeding and leaving a positive impression on their co-workers and customers. They are eager to please, so they are putty in your hands.

But little by little, our dysfunctional workplace cultures chip away at people's spirits and they respond by disengaging. You need to really let this sink in. If organizations had great workplace cultures and managers were trained on how to effectively lead people, we would not be in this predicament. Instead, employees would show up engaged and stay engaged for the duration of their employment.

dysfunctional
[dis-funk-she-nel]
Adjective
1. not operating normally or properly.

Why People Check Out

What are some of the most common reasons why employees disengage? While the list is long, I will call out the top 10 biggest offenders in random order:

1. Poor communication between executives and employees.

2. A lack of purpose or meaning in the work – sometimes, a company's vision doesn't resonate with employees.

3. Employees do not trust executives and their immediate manager.

4. Managers do not take an interest in employees and act like they don't care.

5. Lack of reward and recognition.

6. 'Do as I say, not as I do' executives.

7. Favoritism and a sense that things aren't fair.

8. Lack of accountability (i.e. poor performers are allowed to stay).

9. Lack of respect for employees.

10. Incompetent executives and managers.

As you can see, the vast majority of 'disengagement levers' start with executives and managers. In other words, poor relationships between employees and executives, and between employees and their manager, are a leading cause of employee disengagement.

The good news? Armed with this information, and the strategies in Chapters 7-10, you can turn the situation around and re-engage your most important asset: your employees. Leading and managing people in organizations has taken on new significance this past year. Leadership has never been more difficult, but it also has never been more important.

In Chapter 4, we discussed that people don't quit their jobs; they quit their bosses. Research on employee engagement supports this. Since most people do not like change, many employees choose to stay, but they also choose to add very little value to the organization. While not every disengaged employee is unhappy with his or her manager, many are. And the ones who are, have the potential to be more engaged and productive.

It's important to reiterate that you are not looking for ways to make people happy, but rather, your goal is to find ways to stop employees from being unhappy. Addressing the 10 'disengagement levers' listed above won't lead to immediate engagement, but will start moving employees in the right direction faster than you think. A positive direction.

Why Organizations Have Failed: A Historical Perspective

In life, one of the best ways to move forward and achieve better results is to dissect what you've done, analyzing what worked, what didn't, and why. Many savvy project leaders leverage this strategy at the end of a major initiative by conducting a Postmortem Meeting. This gives a person or team valuable information, so they can repeat what worked and improve upon what didn't work.

> **postmortem**
> [post-more-dem]
> *Adjective*
> 1. an examination of a dead body to determine the cause of death.
> 2. a process intended to help you learn from past incidents; typically involving a blame-free analysis and discussion soon after an event has taken place.

Having researched and analyzed employee engagement statistics, trends, methodologies, failures, and success stories, it's apparent that very little progress has been made. This is because traditional approaches do not move the needle, and yet they are still embraced by the vast majority of organizations.

What is the most popular traditional approach to improve employee engagement? Executives outsource culture change to HR.

This is not a dig against HR. Strategic HR people are wonderful. However, although HR 'owns' culture change in most global organizations, it doesn't 'own' the people who have the greatest impact on the culture in an organization. And who is this? It's you – the managers.

So, in many instances, we see HR roll out employee engagement as a stand-alone program or initiative (think program du jour). With few linkages to the actual business, it's not a priority. Additionally, because HR does not 'own' managers, they usually cannot hold a manager accountable for modifying the way they lead their team. But executives can hold managers accountable and as it relates to employee engagement, this can make all the difference in the world.

Your CEO 'owns' your managers and can get them to do things that HR cannot. For this reason, in order to drive massive improvement in employee engagement, not only do managers need to lead differently, but an executive must champion the journey (more on this in Chapter 11).

> **journey**
> [jer-nee]
> *Noun*
> 1. an American rock band.
> 2. the act of traveling from one place to another, especially when involving a considerable distance.

Is Any Organization Getting It Right?

Although most organizations don't have great cultures, some do. And according to their employees, the company cultures listed below rock. Note that I did not say these organizations are perfect. There are people who dislike these organizations for one reason or another, and who may even attempt to cancel them, thanks to our Cancel Culture. I said their employees love going to work every day and give the culture high marks.

What's different about these organizations? From my research, employees give these employers the shirts off their back because the companies put their people first, so the employees put customers first. This equates to an extraordinary experience, which keeps customers coming back for more. Cha-ching, cha-ching, cha-ching – all the way to the bank.

cha-ching
[cha-chee-ng]
Verb
1. an imitation of the sound that a cash register makes when its drawer is closed after money has been put inside.

What organizations – according to their employees – are currently hitting the ball out of the park? We're talking about companies that employees love and rarely consider leaving. Think:

- Amgen
- Chick-fil-A
- DHL
- Google
- Hilton
- Hulu Beijing
- Mars
- Netflix
- Nordstrom
- Ritz-Carlton Hotel Company
- Royal Plaza on the Scotts
- Salesforce
- SAP
- SAS Institute

- Southwest Airlines
- Zappos
- Zoom Video

These organizations put employees first, so employees can put customers first, and presto – increased employee productivity and retention, customer satisfaction, and profitable revenue growth.

I Believe. So, What's Next?

Now that you understand the future of work, what employee engagement is, the benefits, the dismal state worldwide, and why we are in this position, it's time for us to focus closer to home. In the next chapters, we'll look at your remote team members and their specific needs. Because when you meet an employees' needs, they will be engaged and give you the shirt off their back. Priceless.

CHAPTER 6

What Remoties Say They Need

"It's never overreacting to ask for what you want and need."

– **Amy Poehler** is an American actress, comedian, writer, and director. Poehler has won a Golden Globe Award, Critics' Choice Award, and a Primetime Emmy.

With the COVID-19 pandemic, virtually overnight, many employees and their managers found themselves separated from each other for the first time. From isolation to distractions at home to lack of face-to-face supervision, one of the greatest social experiments of our time had just begun.

Managers were forced to make the transition quickly. But even prior to the pandemic, managing Remoties was not easy. Since the beginning of time, many managers who couldn't 'see' their team members working struggled to trust that their employees were being productive. This is one of the primary reasons why organizations, historically, have shuddered at the thought of adopting a Telecommuting Policy, even though employees clamor for it.

> **productivity**
> [pro-dek-tiv-e-tee]
> *Noun*
> 1. the frequency at which we accomplish tasks, the quality of our output, or how efficient we are.

We've been thrust into a new world of work that is not going away. Regardless of whether your company is working 100 percent remote, hybrid, or 100 percent face-to-face, if you continue to believe that employees who you cannot 'see' working are unproductive, your life as a people leader is going to suck. So, let's spend a bit of time laying out the facts and dispelling this long-held belief.

Productivity = Profit

Productivity is typically measured by an individual's output vs. input over a period of time. However, it's not quite that straight-forward. Some employees produce a high volume of work, but the quality is poor, so other employees must spend time fixing errors.

A more effective way of measuring productivity is to look at a person's output combined with the quality of their work. When we do this, we see that Remoties are more productive at home than they are in an office setting, as long as they are engaged.

> **Stanford**
> [stan-ferd]
> *Noun*
> 1. a private research university in Stanford, California, where really smart people go.

In a Stanford study conducted by Nicholas Bloom, professor in the Department of Economics at Stanford University, and graduate student and founder of Ctrip, James Liang, Ctrip's call center employees were allowed to work from home for nine months.

The results? Remote workers:

- made 13.5 percent more calls than in-office employees.

- reported higher job satisfaction and levels of concentration.

- took fewer sick days, less time off, and shorter breaks.

- demonstrated a productivity boost because they eliminated distractions, like commuting into the office, and changing their work hours to fit their personal schedules.

- logged a turnover rate 50 percent less than in-office employees.

- enabled Ctrip to save on rent, as it reduced the amount of office space needed each month.

Pre-COVID, Airtasker, an Australian outsourcing company, surveyed their full-time employees about their daily work lives. Half of the survey respondents work from home the majority of the week. The key findings?

- Remote employees worked 1.4 days more each month compared to their in-office counterparts, which equates to 16.8 days per year.

- The study found no difference in the quality of work between remote and in-office employees.

- In-office workers were 17 percent more likely to avoid working when their screen time or mouse movements were tracked.

- Remote workers saved an average of $4,523 on fuel each year by eliminating their commutes and reported 25 more minutes of physical activity per week than in-office workers.

- Remote workers saved money on clothes, wear and tear on their car, and lunches, and reported less stress thanks to not having to deal with rush-hour traffic.

Your To Do? Start Anew

Based on the findings in these two studies, and the results of many other remote worker studies, I encourage you to start anew with no preconceived negative beliefs about remote workers. In addition to the fact that negativity will cause you stress and angst, Remoties may pick up on the fact that you do not trust their ability to be productive at home, which will drive disengagement.

> **anew**
> [uh-noo]
> *Adverb*
> 1. in a new or different, and typically more positive, way.

Also, while you may be having a difficult time adjusting to managing employees who you cannot see, it's illogical to think that just because people are physically at the office, they are being productive. We know that most disengaged employees are not productive, and as of this writing, we're talking about 64 percent of U.S. workers and 80 percent of global workers.

Although it may be tempting to continue to believe that you can't trust remote workers to be productive at home, I have a better use for your time. Learn how to manage employees more effectively from a distance and you'll achieve the results you are looking for. This learning process starts with understanding what Remoties need.

The One Thing

When you understand this one thing, effectively managing remote workers will feel less daunting and make a lot of sense to you. So, here it is: if you create a culture where your remote worker's needs are met, they will be productive and give you their all.

culture
[cul-chur]
Noun
1. how we do things here.

I want you to really let that sink in. In other words, if an employee thinks you are making them a priority, they will make you a priority and stay engaged, enthused, and effective. They will give you everything they've got.

And on the flipside, if a worker's needs are not being met, their productivity, loyalty, pride, passion, energy, and engagement will drop. They will give you scraps. It does not matter where an employee sits. What matters is whether the culture in which they are being asked to do their job fulfills their needs.

We're Wired Similarly

You may be thinking that there's no way all of your remote workers have similar needs, since people are different. What I've learned through research, and in life, is that people are not very different. All of your employees are people – human beings – and human beings have very similar needs.

What engages and inspires me, engages and inspires you. What disengages and deflates you, disengages and deflates me. Needs are basically the same, what differs are people's values.

It doesn't matter what industry an employee works in, the country of their residence, or what generation they were born into. People have similar needs. Let me share some evidence to back this up.

Maslow: A Man Ahead of His Time

Maslow's hierarchy of needs is a psychology theory proposed 80 years ago. He created a system, which reflects the universal needs of society at its base, and then proceeds to more acquired emotions. The hierarchy looks at how humans behave and what they need.

> **needs**
> [knee-ds]
> *Adverb*
> 1. of necessity.

Note what Maslow said: "This is what humans need." He didn't say this is what Baby Boomers need, or what people who work in France need, or what people in the Finance industry need. He said this is what all people need. Per the hierarchy, human beings have similar physiological, safety, social, and esteem needs. When all of these needs are met, self-actualization can occur.

What Remoties Need

So, unless you disagree with Maslow, we're on the same page that all human beings have similar needs. Therefore, when researchers interviewed hundreds of thousands of remote workers and they communicated that they need the following Three Cs, it's safe to think the remote workers they didn't talk to also need the Three Cs: Connection, Communication, and Collaboration.

Based on my research, I've added a fourth area to the list of needs: Recognition. Why? Many people feel uncomfortable asking to be acknowledged, but this is a basic need. According to Reward Gateway, a market-leading employee engagement solutions firm, 70 percent of employees say that their motivation, morale, and engagement would improve massively if managers said, "Thank you," more. A simple gesture that will yield enormous returns.

Bottom-line, to get the most out of your remote workers, there are four areas that you need to address. When you get this right, your remote workers will be engaged, enthused, effective, and productive – running on all cylinders – and your life will be easier. Let's dive in.

CHAPTER 7

How to Ace Connection

"I define connection as the energy that exists between people when they feel seen, heard, and valued; when they can give and receive without judgment; and when they derive sustenance and strength from the relationship."

– **Brené Brown** is an American professor, lecturer, author, and podcast host. She is, to date, the author of five No. 1 *New York Times* bestsellers.

When researchers refer to the concept of social connection, they mean the feeling that you belong to a group and feel close to other people. Humans are a social species, so the desire to connect with others is embedded in our biology and evolutionary history. Connection is a core psychological need. When we are born, deep connections form within seconds; the first being our mother or caregiver.

Neuroscientist Matthew Lieberman writes in his book, *Social: Why Our Brains Are Wired to Connect,* "This is what our brains were wired for: reaching out to and interacting with others. These social adaptations are central to making us the most successful species on earth."

brain
[bray-n]
Noun
1. the most complex part of the human body. This three-pound organ is the seat of intelligence, interpreter of the senses, initiator of body movement, and controller of behavior.

So, it stands to reason that social connection at work is not only a need, but a very crucial component in building a productive, engaged, and efficient workplace. Connected teams collaborate more often, provide support for the team members, are more creative, and have healthier working relationships.

Unfortunately, organizations are not doing a great job fulfilling this need for employees. According to the *Harvard Business Review*, even prior to the Pandemic, 40 percent of employees felt lonely at work. Certainly, social distancing has caused that number to grow, and the impact on your team members and their productivity can be enormous.

Why Connection is Critical

Why is it so important for you to get your arms around this and improve it? Because the definition of an engaged employee is someone who trusts their leaders and feels an emotional connection to the organization. This feeling of connection is actually necessary in order for employees to be engaged, enthused, and effective. If your people feel disconnected, they will begin to disengage. And it's not even a choice that an employee will make – it will happen subconsciously because they have an unmet need.

subconscious
[sub-con-shes]
Adjective
1. the part of the mind of which one is not fully aware, but which influences one's actions and feelings.

People are motivated by the deeply human need to direct their lives, and make a difference for themselves, others, and the world around them. This reality holds true for all of your employees, regardless of their age, and especially for Generation Z and Millennials.

Generations in the Workplace

- Generation Z (born between 1997–2012)
- Millennials (1981–1996)
- Generation Xers (1965–1980)
- Baby Boomers (1946–1964)
- Silent Generation (1928–1945)

Multinational professional services firm Price Waterhouse Coopers estimates that by the end of 2025, Gen Zs and Millennials will form 75 percent of the global workforce. Far more vocal than people in other generations, they refuse to be a thought of as simply a number or a cog in the wheel. If you don't give them what they need, they'll simply quit. Imagine the impact on your business if three-quarters of your workforce resigned because you are not fulfilling their need for connection.

Anti-Social Media

To make matters worse, we live in strangely disconnected times. The Internet and social media promised to deliver new forms of connectedness, but social media is anything but social. Anti-social is more like it.

We sit alone engaging with technology, which has created a greater sense of disconnectedness. This impacts our happiness, friendships, relationships, communities, and self-esteem, both inside and outside of our workplaces. Technology should be enhancing our connection to others, but instead, it's replacing it.

social media
[so-shul mee-dee-uh]
Noun
1. interactive technologies that allow the sharing/exchange of information and ideas via virtual communities.
2. organizations that typically support the Cancel Culture and wield ridiculous amounts of power.

Humans have an innate need to be connected to something bigger than themselves, have meaning, add value, and make a difference. And we're learning the hard way that when you physically disperse people, this sense of connection diminishes.

One of the unfortunate byproducts of this disconnectedness is the lost art of conversation. The generations that have grown up playing online video games have become less capable of effective verbal communication, and worse, many of them don't recognize it.

COVID-19 Strikes Again

Within several months of the March 2020 COVID-19 lockdown, the vast majority of my neighbors and friends working from home said to me, "I cannot believe how disconnected and isolated I feel from my workplace co-workers." There's something about being physically co-located with other people that fulfills the need most people have to be a part of something bigger than themself. To be connected.

A great example of this is a live concert or sporting event. Think about the last time you attended a large, energy-filled event with tens of thousands of other people, who were actually strangers. You didn't know one another. But when the performer sang his or her uplifting No. 1 song, or the larger-than-life athlete scored, you felt this deep sense of camaraderie and connection with thousands of people who were physically around you – and you didn't even know them.

This happened because you were all moved by the same thing. You all felt a part of something bigger than yourself.

And it fulfilled your need for connection. But with remote working, we've lost that. So, in the absence of being physically connected to one another, you must create that connection in other ways.

What You Can Do as a Leader

How can you fill the need your employees have for connection? Here are seven proven ideas to consider, that will enable your team members to get to know one another on a personal level, which will increase the sense of connection they feel:

1. **Pair People in Twos.**
   Create a Buddy/Support System for every remote worker, so your people have someone to turn to, rely on, vent to, etc. Ask people if they would like to select several employees who they'd like to be partnered with (and then you decide who to pair with whom) or if they would like to be paired up randomly.

2. **Virtual Happy Hour with a Topic of the Week.**
   Everyone can provide their own beverage, or you could purchase small to-go Cocktail Kits on Amazon and have them shipped to people's homes. Also, select a fun – non-work related – topic to discuss in advance and ask each team member to share their thoughts.

3. **Troop Tour/Show & Tell.**
   Have employees lead a video tour of their home workspace. Include a Show & Tell portion, so employees can share something in their home office and talk about why its meaningful to them. Note: Some people may not be proud of their home workspace, so give employees the option of doing the Show & Tell portion only.

4. **Team Goal.**
   One of the easiest ways to make people feel connected is to create a team goal that everyone is responsible for achieving together. This goal will be especially powerful if it's in support of one of your CEO's goals. When you create a team goal aligned to the vision of the CEO, people will feel they are walking together arm in arm toward the same North Star – connected to something bigger than themselves.

5. **Mini-Book of Bios.**
   Ask your team members to send you old photos, fun facts, their retirement vision, childhood dreams, a description of their best friend, personal and professional achievements, etc. Compile this information on an intranet page or into a PDF document and share it with your team. Then lead a Q&A session, where people can dig deeper and ask questions.

6. **Recognition Roundtable.**
   Set-up a standing weekly or monthly video conference, where everyone acknowledges someone on the team. As the team leader, you could also mail a gift to employees for this regular event, such as balloons, a gift card for lunch, a hand-written thank you note, a snack box, or a coupon for a Late Start or Early Finish.

7. **Role & Soul.**
   Host a get together where employees explain their role on the team and why their job lights up their soul – why they love their job. By reflecting on and sharing this information, your team members will be on a path of learning how to connect more deeply with both themselves and others. In the words of Aristotle, "Knowing yourself is the beginning of all wisdom."

Although not all of these ideas may suit your team, they will bring fun into the workplace and enable your team members to get to know one another on a more personal level. Research tells us that when colleagues know one another on both a work level and a personal level, they feel a deeper sense of connection to the team and to the organization. And more importantly, a critical need that your Remoties have – Connection – will be fulfilled.

Next up? The critical art of communication.

CHAPTER 8

How to Ace Communication

*"It's about communication. It's about honesty.
It's about treating people as deserving to know the facts.
You don't give them half the story. You don't hide
the story. You treat them as true equals, and you
communicate, communicate, communicate."*

– **Louis Gerstner,** an American businessman best known
for his tenure as former chairman of the board
and CEO of IBM. He is credited with turning
IBM's fortunes around.

Another major need of virtual workers? Communication.

As we discussed earlier, Price Waterhouse Coopers estimates that by the end of 2025, Gen Zs and Millennials will form 75 percent of the global workforce. People in these generations were born with a Smartphone in their hand. They bombard people with communications and are comfortable being bombarded with communications. They don't know any other way. It's a part of their culture.

And then Gen Zs and Millennials enter the workforce and hear from the CEO once a year. Or their manager does not hold regular staff meetings. Or major decisions are made with no input from employees – the people who will be directly impacted. And then we sit back and wonder why employees disengage. Really?

disengage
[dis-en-gaj]
Verb
1. to separate or release (someone or something) from something to which they are attached or connected.

Employees say that when they are kept in the loop about what is going on, when they have a voice at work, and think their voice is being heard, their employee engagement increases. When senior leaders and managers share information and seek out the thoughts, ideas, opinions, hopes, and wishes of employees, in return, it causes them to trust leaders and feel an emotional connection to the organization – the definition of employee engagement.

Old Needs Call for New Solutions

It's important to note that communication is not a new need that workers now have. It's a need that has been unfulfilled long before COVID-19.

I have analyzed the Employee Engagement Survey results for companies in more than 33 industries. Interestingly, the same handful of questions land in the 'five lowest scoring questions' virtually every time. One of them is: Communications between senior leaders and employees is good.

unfortunate
[un-four-chew-nut]
Adjective
1. having or marked by bad fortune; unlucky.

From my experience, this question scores between 10 percent and 30 percent positive in most organizations. This is unfortunate when you consider the fact that the benefits of effective communication are vast:

- Fosters trust with others.
- Prevents or resolves problems.
- Provides clarity and direction.
- Creates better relationships.
- Improves productivity.
- Promotes team building.
- Increases engagement.

Communication is Not Created Equal

Before we dive into ways that you can ensure you meet your employee's communication needs, let's consider the types of communication cultures that exist in organizations and the one you should aim to create:

- In a **No-Way Communication Culture**, communications between senior leaders and employees are virtually non-existent. This leads to employees having to guess what the goal is, and middle managers who have to make things up. Needless to say, these cultures disengage employees and are incredibly dysfunctional because one hand does not know what the other hand is doing. Also, there is a great lack of trust.

- In a **One-Way Communication Culture**, communications between senior leaders and employees are just that: all one way. Information is pushed out to employees, but people rarely have the opportunity to chime in, voice their opinion, ask questions, or get clarity about something they do not understand. These cultures also disengage employees because people want to have a voice at work and know their voice is being heard.

- In a **Two-Way Communication Culture** – by far and obviously the most effective – communications between senior leaders and employees are frequent, honest, and open. Information is disseminated to employees, and people have the opportunity to engage in a dialogue or conversation with managers and/or senior leaders about the information. These cultures engage employees because they give people the opportunity to have a voice at work and be heard.

While I'm not advocating that everything should be passed by employees for their opinion or for a vote (that's obviously unproductive as nothing would get done), I am confident there are more opportunities for you to engage in a dialogue with employees than you are taking advantage of.

What You Can Do as a Leader

So, how can you fill the need your employees have for open, honest, timely, two-way communication? Here are seven proven ideas that will enable the lines to be open and flowing in both directions:

1. **Face-to-Face Rules.**
   Opt for video meetings (camera on) and phone calls vs. texts and emails. Face-to-face communication demonstrates importance, makes it easier to interpret thoughts and feelings, and enhances credibility and trust. If this is not possible, pick up the phone. Leverage texts for quick reminders and emails when details need to be documented.

2. **Team Huddle.**
   Lead a daily or weekly huddle. Invite all employees to attend and make it voluntary. If your huddle is in the a.m., ask people to share what's on their plates that day and what they may need help with. A p.m. huddle is a great opportunity for you to ask employees, "What was your best accomplishment today?" and end the workday on a high note.

3. **One-on-Ones.**
   Managers say they don't conduct monthly one-on-ones with their direct reports because they don't know what to talk about. Therefore, brainstorm one question each month and have it be the topic of all of your one-on-ones. For instance: "How can I help you now that we are remote?" "What do you like and dislike about your job?" "What form of recognition do you like best?"

4. **Success Bulletins.**
   Publicly celebrate the successes your company, team, and team members have using Success Bulletins that are distributed to everyone. People love to be on a winning team and be surrounded by winners, so don't always wait for the next scheduled update to communicate a success. These bulletins will act as great culture and morale boosters.

5. **Rotate Leadership of Staff Meetings.**
   Conduct a weekly staff meeting led by a different team member each week. Why? Because when you ask Kim to lead next week's staff meeting, do you know what Kim just heard? My manager trusts me. And this leads to Kim trusting you more. Also, it enables Kim to act in a leadership role and do the majority of the talking during the meeting, which will positively impact the flow of communication, since people communicate more easily with peers than leaders.

6. **Suggestions Email Box.**
   Give remote workers an avenue to provide feedback about their remote office experience and recommend ideas as to how to improve it. The employee who submits the best monthly idea receives recognition and their idea is implemented.

The Suggestions Box enables people to have a voice and enables you to improve the experience, which will increase employee engagement.

7. **Focus Groups.**

When an important decision needs to be made that impacts people, ask for their input prior to making the decision. You can gather input via Focus Groups, where you bring together eight to 15 people, and ask for their thoughts and opinions prior to making a decision. Then when you announce the decision, say, "You spoke, I listened," and explain why you made the decision you did. This is called 'creating context' and it will go a long way toward heading off questions.

trenches
[tren-chez]
Noun
1. a long, narrow ditch.
2. a system of excavations used for the protection of troops.

Your employees are in the trenches – they are closest to your customer. They likely know much more about what's going on in your business, have creative ideas about how to fix what's broken, thoughts about how to generate additional revenue and cut expenses, and ideas about what your next product or service should be. They also often have a great perspective on how your company and its offerings stack up against the competition.

If you don't seek out employee's thoughts, you'll never tap into this wealth of information. And you'll breed active disengagement because people need communication. They want to know what's going on and they want to engage in a dialogue about the content. Embrace these ideas and you will be well on your way to building a two-way communication culture that people can't imagine leaving.

Next up? How to ace collaboration – the third critical need of your Remoties. As a leader of people, it's your responsibility to seek out and implement ideas that enable your team members to engage in group work. No team runs successfully without collaboration, so let's dive in.

CHAPTER 9

How to Ace Collaboration

"I can do things you cannot, you can do things I cannot; together we can do great things."

– **Mother Teresa** was an Albanian-Indian Roman Catholic nun and missionary. Teresa received a number of honors, including a Nobel Peace Prize, and is admired by many for her charitable work.

Thanks to COVID-19, many employees are now alone in their home office working in isolation. So, it's not surprising that people are clamoring for opportunities to collaborate. A learned skill, collaboration is basically group work – people coming together to contribute their expertise for the benefit of a shared objective, project, or mission.

According to Benjamin Jones, a strategy professor at the Kellogg School, collaboration is more important now than ever because our individual knowledge base is becoming incredibly specialized. "There's more and more to know in the world, and you can only have so much in your head," Jones says. "Therefore, the share of stuff that any one individual knows is declining in every field."

collaboration
[ko-lab-er-a-shen]
Noun
1. two or more people, entities, or organizations working together to complete a task or achieve a goal.

The Keys to the Kingdom

What are other key reasons why collaboration is important?

- **Collaboration Helps People Problem-Solve**
  When working, it's not unusual to get stumped, to not know what to do next, to encounter a

roadblock, or to feel lost. One of the most effective ways to move forward is to seek out the perspective of another individual, or a group of people. When people pool their knowledge, skills, and expertise, and then talk problems through and debate potential solutions, stalled projects begin to move forward again.

- **Collaboration Helps People Be More Efficient**
When employees face something that is complex and overwhelming, they have three choices: give up, push through slowly on their own, or seek out help from others to succeed. Collaboration helps employees divide up a heavy workload, find creative solutions to tough problems, and execute a solution much quicker than they would have if they were working alone.

- **Collaboration Helps People Grow**
People bring different skill sets and backgrounds to the table. Collaboration enables employees to tap into – and learn from – the diverse experiences, insights, mistakes, and successes, of others. Ultimately, these learnings and epiphanies can alter the way someone thinks going forward, which can be extremely valuable to your team.

- **Collaboration Boosts Employee Engagement and Morale**
  As connections are made between people, teams, and departments, trust will increase, which boosts employee morale and engagement. Partnering with someone and realizing success together is one of the most effective ways to build trust. Additionally, as employee morale and engagement increase, people will feel more comfortable working alongside others and seek out opportunities to collaborate on their own.

- **Collaboration Increases Employee Retention**
  Collaboration lays the foundation for an open, engaged workplace, which values teamwork. This is much more appealing to both current and future employees than an organization that operates in silos and is disconnected. A work environment where collaboration is a priority will go a long way toward preventing employees from looking for a new job or from being cherry-picked by a competitor.

- **Collaboration Opens Up New Communication Channels**
  The success of a business, in part, relies on having clear information that is easy to find, and accessible to everyone who has a need to know. Collaboration

tools, such as an intranet, do just that. They open up your business, so everyone in the organization can communicate with one another and know what other teams do and are working on.

> **benefits**
> [ben-eh-fits]
> *Noun*
> 1. an advantage or profit gained from something.

What You Can Do as a Leader

Now that you understand the benefits, what can you do to fulfill the need that remote workers have for increased collaboration? Here are seven proven ideas:

1. **Delegate to Everyone.**
   There's a phenomenon that happens in life where the same people are chosen again and again to lead. It's called the Halo Effect and needless to say, it disengages employees who are never selected, causing them to feel deflated and be less productive. You must trust all of your remote workers to collaborate on and execute high-profile projects; not just your high performers. Spread the wealth around. Select new people to collaborate and fix a problem or lead a major project, and then give them a runway to 'get the job done.'

2. **Team Building Games.**

   Fun team building activities are important to the success of your business. The personal bonds formed between team members give your company a competitive edge, help build new relationships, and teach people to work together effectively. These activities and other problem-solving games are also an effective way to teach employees to trust one another's judgment, problem-solve in a group, and communicate more effectively. Thousands of ideas can be found on the Internet.

3. **Online Collaboration Tools.**

   One of the best ways to increase team collaboration is with team collaboration software. These platforms store, share, and train via videos, documents, and video conferences. With a simple search, an employee can find the right information or person from across the world, and converse about internal tasks, group activities, policy changes, challenges, ideas, questions, and more. Be a role model – use your firms' online tool and if you don't have one, speak with IT about getting one.

4. **Team Charter.**

   A Team Charter is a living document that serves as a North Star for a team or project. Ask your team members to collaborate and develop a Charter that outlines the team's purpose, mission, goals, Key Performance Indicators (KPIs), and the roles people are expected to play in order to achieve the goals. The Team Charter can also include the team hierarchy, structure, and values, which will give people direction and boundaries.

5. **Team Innovations Meeting.**
Lead a monthly or quarterly meeting where your team members generate as many ideas as possible, design or redesign a process, or develop an entirely new approach for your team. The meeting format should rely on rapid brainstorming to get your team's creativity flowing and transform people into innovators. Once the team votes and decides what to pursue first, allot time for employees to actually focus on the tasks at hand. Then give team members a runway to collaborate and don't forget to celebrate the successes.

6. **Mind the Time and Zone.**
In order for people and teams to collaborate more easily, you must ensure 100 percent participation in meetings. You will accomplish this if you are aware of your meeting times; and if you lead a distributed team, the various time zones of all team members. According to a study conducted by YouCanBookMe, a U.K.-based scheduling firm,

the most optimal time to book a meeting is on Tuesday at 2:30 p.m. If you lead a team located across different time zones, you can find the best time with the *https://www.timeanddate.com* World Clock Meeting Planner.

7. **Reward Collaboration.**

   A workplace truism? You get more of what you reward. When employees who collaborate effectively are held up as role models and acknowledged, other employees will collaborate in an effort to be rewarded. Recognize, acknowledge, and celebrate collaboration – and the team's successes – and your people will naturally do it more often.

responsibility
[reh-spons-uh-bill-i-tee]
Noun
1. the state or fact of having a duty to deal with something or of having control over someone.

What could be more beneficial for your business than a strong team of professionals who know their work? A strong team of professionals who collaborate. As a leader of people, it's your responsibility to seek out and implement ideas that enable your team members to engage in group work. No team runs successfully without collaboration, so execute on the ideas in this Chapter and you will have met three of your remote worker's needs.

The fourth need? It's not one Remoties say they need, but trust me when I say that they do. Employee recognition plays a pivotal role in increasing employee engagement and satisfaction, so let's dive in. Once you ace recognition, you will be well on your way to building a team of remote employees who run on all cylinders and give you 100 percent discretionary effort – the secret sauce to awesome business results.

CHAPTER 10

How to Ace Recognition

"The deepest desire of the human spirit is to be acknowledged."

– **Stephen Covey,** was an American educator, author, businessman, and keynote speaker. His most popular book is *The 7 Habits of Highly Effective People*, and *Time* magazine named him one of the 25 most influential people.

In Chapter 6, we established that all human beings have similar physiological, safety, social, and esteem needs. And when all of these needs are met, self-actualization can occur.

Therefore, when researchers interviewed hundreds of thousands of remote workers and the employees communicated that they need the Three Cs – Connection, Communication, and Collaboration – it's safe to think the remote workers they didn't talk to also need the Three Cs.

However, I believe Remoties left a critical need off the list – recognition. Why? Many people feel uncomfortable asking to be acknowledged and appreciated for their hard work, and contributions to an organization. We know from research that appropriate recognition fuels employee's motivation, retention, productivity, morale, and engagement, so you'd be smart to add it to the Three Cs.

recognition
[rek-eg-nich-en]
Noun
1. the acknowledgement of a person's behavior, effort, or result that supports the organization's goals and values, and exceeds normal expectations.

As Opera Winfrey concluded in her Harvard University commencement address, "I have done 35,000 interviews in my career. As soon as the camera shuts off, everyone turns to me and inevitably asks, 'Was that OK?' I heard it from former U.S. President Bush. I heard it from former U.S. President Obama. I've heard it from heroes and housewives. I've heard it from victims and criminals. I even heard it from Beyoncé. She finishes performing, hands me the microphone and says, 'Was that OK?' They all want to know one thing: Was that OK?"

Employee feedback and recognition answers this fundamental question – "Was that OK?" – in an employer/employee relationship.

Numbers Don't Lie; However, Some Politicians Do

In addition to inspiring employees to run on all cylinders and give you a lot of discretionary effort, consider these critical data points about employee recognition, which is a whopping $46 billion market worldwide:

- 90 percent of employees who received thanks or recognition from their boss report feeling high levels of trust in that individual. (*Forbes*)

- 85 percent of employees are satisfied with a simple, "Thank you," for their daily efforts and accomplishments. (Deloitte)

- 69 percent of employees would work harder if they felt their efforts were better appreciated. (Socialcast)

- 63 percent of appropriately recognized employees are highly unlikely to quit their jobs. (SurveyMonkey)

- 58 percent of employees replied "give recognition" when asked what leaders could do more of to improve engagement. (Vantage Circle)

- 40 percent of employees state that receiving recognition more often would encourage them to do more work. (*Harvard Business Review*)

Although the case is clear for employee recognition, 82 percent of employed Americans – 63 percent globally – don't feel that their supervisors recognize them enough for their contributions.

And according to Bersin & Associates, 87 percent of recognition programs focus on tenure, which is not appropriate recognition, as it rewards quantity vs. quality. It is far better to focus workplace compliments on professional qualities, such as someone's attitude, skills, talents, values, qualities, or contributions.

However, even when you recognize people correctly, it can land on people as wrong.

Are You Talking to Me?

Although most people like hearing praise, some people bristle when they hear compliments. According to *Psychology Today*, "Our receptivity to compliments is a reflection of our self-esteem and feelings of self-worth. Compliments can make people with low self-esteem feel uncomfortable because the kind words contradict their own self-views."

In one study, college students with low self-esteem elected to keep their current roommate if that roommate viewed them negatively rather than if their roommate viewed them positively. We tend to seek out people who validate the opinion we have about ourselves.

> **bristle**
> [bris-el]
> *Noun*
> 1. to show sudden anger or other negative response to something.
> 2. a short stiff hair, typically on an animal's skin, a man's face, or a plant.

Even if everyone on your team has self-confidence, recognition is something you are going to have to work at because giving people compliments does not come naturally to most people.

Consider the following.

Welcome to Complaints Central

We live in a world where many people would rather focus on issues and complain than compliment someone. Maybe this explains how I discovered a popular Salesforce article titled, *10 Effective Ways to Complain About a Company Online*, which chronicles the most effective ways to file complaints that a company will pay attention to. Welcome to Complaints Central – your one stop resource for complaint contacts, information, and tips to get heard.

The average person is said to complain 15-30 times a day. According to Will Bowen, author of *A Complaint Free World*, there are five main reasons why people complain: to establish camaraderie, avoid taking action by shirking responsibility, brag about their superiority, control others, and pre-excuse poor performance, behavior, or inaction.

But even though we live in a world dominated by complainers, the need that people have to be recognized is alive and well.

Calling All Robots

According to the *Harvard Business Review*, people crave praise so much that they respond to it even from a robot. After warning signs and live video monitors were placed by hand sanitizer stations in hospitals, only 10 percent of employees were washing their hands. When electronic systems were installed that gave immediate praise for hand washing, the rate of compliance jumped to 90 percent.

robot
[row-bot]
Noun
1. a machine resembling a human being and able to replicate certain human movements and functions automatically.

While compliments from actual human beings are obviously more relevant and meaningful than those from robots, this research shows the power of our need to be praised for good behavior. And, when you ensure the recognition is sincere, timely, and specific, you'll really hit a home run with your team members.

S-T-S: The Golden Ticket

The key to rewarding people well is that the recognition must be S-T-S: Sincere, Timely, and Specific. Sending an impersonal group email that says, "Great job," with no context, to an entire team days after a major product launch is going to fall flat and not have the desired impact.

Face-to-face recognition, a phone call, a personalized email, or a hand-written note will be exponentially more impactful as a means to deliver positive feedback and recognition. In addition to being cognizant of the medium you use, your efforts also have to feel personal and genuine for them to be well-received.

- **Be Sincere**
  The most important part of saying "thank you" is being sincere. People are smart. If you thank them out of obligation, they'll know. Speak confidently, showing that you mean every word you say, and be honest. Open up and speak from your heart.

- **Be Timely**
  It's more effective to offer the praise as close to the timing of the event as possible vs. waiting days or weeks to thank the employee. When an employee is thanked in real-time, especially publicly in front of their peers, it re-enforces the positive behaviors that the employee exhibited, and can motivate others. Success Bulletins are an easy way to accomplish this.

- **Be Specific**
  When recognizing an employee, content is king. The recognition must be specific to the person and highlight his/her role in the accomplishment. When people are praised for something specific, it increases the likelihood that they will repeat the behavior.

Finally, don't underestimate the effectiveness of repetition. Recognition is one of the greatest human needs. Therefore, when it occurs on a regular basis, it will help create an environment that people love, where they can soar, so your team and company meet or exceed its goals. Doling out recognition is a simple and inexpensive way to fuel employees forward.

Proud of Your Work/Proud of Your Company Inspires Greatness

Now let's consider the all-important recognition programs. According to the CEO of WorkProud.com, Michael Levy, "More than 80 percent of recognition programs deployed are either poorly delivered or emphasize the wrong things. There are three common pitfalls that companies fall into."

1. The quality and execution of recognition programs is weak. Employees have been raised on high-end social media platforms, such as Facebook, Instagram, Tic-Toc, Slack, and Microsoft Teams. In order to create comparably valued experiences, the program must be high-quality, contemporary, and automated vs. manual.

2. Old-school paper-based processes don't fit our modern world. Many companies still cling to outdated approaches for handling their recognition processes. Sending paper-based cards alone does

not work in a global, digital, remote world. You need an online solution as well. While a hand-written note has great value, it shouldn't be the core of your recognition solution. Leverage technology.

3. Overemphasis on the value of monetary awards. While gift cards, points, and prizes have a valuable and important role to play, they must be built upon a foundation of non-monetary recognition. Layered programs with non-monetary, monetary, and symbolic recognition (i.e. public/ formal accolades) elements have the biggest impact.

As Levy often says, inspired by some of Jack Welch's principles of leadership, "Create an atmosphere and culture, where employees feel Proud of Their Work and Proud of Their Company, and they will be inspired to consistently give their best."

Take It to the Next Level

While I'm about to share ideas to create an environment of rampant recognition on your team, the truth is that each person will respond to and prefer different types of recognition. So, if you want to tailor recognition to individual employees, simply ask everyone how they would prefer to be recognized.

rampant
[ram-pent]
Adjective
1. marked by a menacing wildness, extravagance, or absence of restraint.

The more you get to know your employees, the better you'll understand how to recognize them. If they appear uncomfortable, try a different form of recognition the next time. The most important element is that no matter what type of recognition you currently give, a good place to start is by simply giving more.

What You Can Do as a Leader

According to Globoforce, only 14 percent of organizations provide managers with the necessary tools – and budget – for reward and recognition. So, here are seven proven virtual appreciation ideas that will enable your Remoties to feel acknowledged, appreciated, inspired, and motivated:

1. **Thank You.**
   Nothing says "Thank you" more than spoken words or a hand-written card. Nothing. Remember, 85 percent of employees say they are satisfied with a simple, "Thank you," for their daily efforts and accomplishments. This is one of the most personal

ways to show your appreciation, and the effort
you put into crafting your sentiment will be
apparent when you add what you are thanking
the employee for.

2. **Virtual Gratitude Channel.**
A Gratitude Channel is a place online where your
team members are encouraged to post messages
to thank co-workers for their daily efforts and
celebrate their successes. As the team leader,
randomly select one post each week and recognize
both the giver and the receiver with a reward.

3. **Pet Project.**
Ask your team members to bring their pet to work
remotely. They can show their pet to co-workers
and recognize the animal for its unique qualities.
If someone does not have a pet, they can feature a
child or significant other (even via a photograph).

4. **Recognition Roundtable.**
Peer recognition is powerful; it doesn't always have
to come from the boss. Set-up a standing monthly
video conference, where everyone acknowledges
someone on the team. The only Ground Rules?
Sincere, Timely, and Specific.

5. **Rooftop Shout Out.**
One of the best ways to recognize employees is to
spread the word about noteworthy individual and

team accomplishments during large-group meetings, in emails to your entire company, and on social media. Explain why you are so proud, how the achievement impacts the bigger picture, and tag all team members. People work harder when they know their work makes a difference.

6. **Remote Employee Appreciation Day.**
Allocate a quarterly budget for gift boxes, recognition program reward points, Late Start/ Early Finish coupons, Cocktail Kits, and Time Off vouchers. In the meeting, start by giving virtual kudos to the team as a whole. Then go through the individual names and rewards systematically.

7. **Online-Rewards/Points Program.**
Employees grant one another points for living the values, achieving goals, and going above and beyond the call of duty. After accumulating a certain number of points, employees can redeem them for gifts and experiences from an online catalogue. A top performer in this space? *https://workproud.com.* It's smart technology that aligns your values and goals with employee's needs, and the user interface is a key driver for success.

The data tells us that recognition will inspire your people to trust you more, work harder, stay longer, be more engaged, have pride in your workplace, and do more work. And most importantly, a critical need that your Remoties have – Recognition – will be fulfilled. Now let's bring this all together, so you can execute on it successfully in your day-to-day world.

CHAPTER 11

Your Strategy for Success

"Action is the foundational key to all success."

– **Pablo Picasso** was a Spanish painter, sculptor, printmaker, ceramicist, and theatre designer. Picasso is regarded as one of the most influential artists of the 20th century.

My goal is to make things simple, so you can succeed. As I communicated in the opening Important Notes, this book was written for managers, so they can do a better job engaging their remote team members. However, as previously stated, the ideas presented can also be used by business owners, senior leaders, business units or department heads, or HR professionals to engage every remote worker in an organization.

These simple, straight-forward solutions work for a five-person team or a 250,000-person organization. Why? Because remote workers are human beings and most human beings are wired similarly.

Here is your roadmap for success – how this all comes together in your day-to-day world – whether you are a manager implementing the strategy on your team or a leader implementing it across an entire organization.

I'm a Manager: Implementing on My Team

Step 1. Plan
Look at the lists in Chapters 7-10, which contain 28 ideas to engage remote workers. Think of the lists as a restaurant menu. You would not go to a restaurant and order 28 items, just as you will not execute on all 28 ideas. Review the lists

and choose two or three ideas from each area that you think will be most effective with your team, and which you are most comfortable doing. Most of the ideas can also be used in a hybrid environment, with employees who are not remote. The most important thing is that you consistently execute on several ideas in each area: Connection, Communication, Collaboration, and Recognition.

Step 2. Execute
Once you have chosen the ideas you are going to implement, it's up to you to execute. Execution done right is a disciplined process. Most businesspeople fail at execution due to the lack of a repeatable framework or methodology. For instance, if you are going to lead a weekly Team Huddle or monthly Team Innovations Meeting, send out a calendar invite for a year's worth of meetings. Commit. If you are going to give your team members hand-written recognition notes, put an event on your calendar for the end of each workday to recognize a team member. You get the picture.

Step 3. Measure
Keeping tabs on your progress is key to ensuring you're on the right track, and helps keep performance aligned with the plan. A simple way to track engagement is to ask remote workers one question every Friday: Would you recommend our team as a great place to work? Your "Yes" respondents are engaged, your "I don't know" respondents are neither

engaged nor disengaged, and your "No" respondents are disengaged. This enables you to track the sentiments of your remote workers in real time, so you know if you are making progress or if you need to course correct. Your goal is to steadily increase engagement month over month, quarter over quarter, year over year.

I'm a Leader: Implementing Across an Entire Organization

Step 1. Share

This content needs to be put into the hands of your managers, so they can execute on it in the trenches with the employees on their teams. The most effective way to do this is to hold Manager Town Hall Meetings, where you bring managers together virtually. In a perfect world, a senior leader would lead your Manager Town Hall Meetings. Why? Because when senior leaders speak, people listen. During these meetings, you will discuss the benefits of keeping remote workers engaged, share the 28 ideas to engage remote workers, communicate how progress will be measured, and field concerns, questions, etc.

Step 2. Guide

Guide managers to look at the lists in Chapters 7-10, which contain the 28 ideas, and to think of the lists as a restaurant menu. Remind managers that they would not go to a restaurant and order 28 items, just as they will not execute on all

28 ideas. Advise them to review the lists and choose two or three ideas from each area that they think will be most effective with their team, and which they are most comfortable doing. Most of the ideas can also be used in a hybrid environment, with employees who are not remote. The most important thing is that they consistently execute on several ideas in each area: Connection, Communication, Collaboration, and Recognition.

Step 3. Execute

Once each manager chooses the ideas they are going to implement, it's up to them to execute. Communicate that execution done right is a disciplined process. Most managers fail at execution due to the lack of a repeatable framework or methodology. For instance, if they are going to lead a weekly Team Huddle or monthly Team Innovations Meeting, recommend that they send out a calendar invite for a year's worth of meetings. If they are going to give their team members hand-written recognition notes, recommend that they put an event on their calendar for the end of each workday.

Step 4. Measure

Here are two options to measure your manager's performance and ensure they are executing on the action items. I recommend you use one of following:

- Use your current Employee Engagement Survey to track the sentiments of remote workers. Add one question to your survey asking people to identify their work location. 'Ihis will enable you to run the Survey results of remote workers only, and see if you are trending up or down.

- If you don't have an Employee Engagement Survey, ask remote workers to respond to one statement every week: I would recommend my company as a great place to work. Your "Yes" respondents are engaged, your "I don't know" respondents are neither engaged nor disengaged, and your "No" respondents are disengaged. This enables you to track the sentiments of your remote workers in real time, so you know if your managers are making progress or if they need to course correct. Then, circle back with managers and share the results with them. Your goal should be to steadily increase engagement month over month, quarter over quarter, year over year.

One Last Thing

While it might be tempting to rest on your laurels and think that your employees are going to stay in your organization thanks to the fact that many people don't like change, I encourage you to think again. If an employee's needs are not being met, they will disengage, check out, and some will also tender their resignation notice ... because they can. Employees still have options. And truthfully? They have more options today than they've ever had. Many organizations that historically only hired people who live in the company's city or state are now launching national and even global candidate searches thanks to the fact that remote work is here to stay.

Additionally, thousands of organizations with great workplace cultures are hiring, and it's usually not your low performers who leave. High performers leave because they have courage, self-confidence, know their worth, and trust they can write their own ticket. And they are right.

You have a choice: do nothing and risk productivity, performance, and profitability, or embark on a journey to engage your Remoties.

The definition of culture is how we do things here. To improve a team or organizational culture, managers simply need to do things here differently – and better – tomorrow then they are doing today. It's that straightforward.

Employee engagement is not difficult. By following the game plan in this book, you will create an environment that virtual workers love because it meets their needs, which will inspire them to be the best version of themselves every day.

The result? People who give you a lot of discretionary effort, which is the secret sauce to extraordinary business results. When employees are engaged, their No. 1 objective is to contribute to the company's success.

People simply want to know you care. They want to feel connected to something bigger than themselves. They want to have a voice and know their voice is being heard. They want to partner with their co-workers to make a difference. They want to be acknowledged for a job well done.

Sometimes, however, despite your best efforts to implement a successful employee engagement strategy, some employees just won't respond. At this point, partner with these people to develop them, and if they still do not respond, terminate them. If a person simply won't engage, they will pollute your culture and your efforts may fail. Separate them from the company for your sake and the sake of your other team members.

If you cannot separate a disengaged employee thanks to their status or government regulations, you must minimize their exposure. Put them in a role where they have as little interaction with others as possible and make sure they do not lead people.

Tackle remote worker management with confidence, courage, and optimism. And along the journey, have fun. Because I can assure you that if you aren't deliberate about creating an extraordinary culture that meets people's needs, you will end up with a culture by chance. And it will not be pretty; it will be mediocre at best, and we all know that mediocrity does not breed business success.

> **fun**
> fuh-nun
> *Noun*
> 1. enjoyment, amusement, or lighthearted pleasure.

When you make remote workers a priority, you will see measurable results, and your key stakeholders will be grateful they have a leader in their midst. And more importantly, you will know you've made a difference in the lives of the people who yearn for real leadership. Now that's what I call success.

And finally, it's critical for you to remember that employee engagement efforts are not a snapshot item, but a motion picture. One-time efforts are not sufficient; it takes a sustained and consistent effort to succeed. This is a journey, not a sprint. But one I know you will ace.

Why? You chose to pick up this book and read it. That tells me you recognize the need, you 'get it', and for this I applaud you. Never ever doubt yourself, or your ability to meet or exceed your Remoties' needs and your employee engagement goals. You have everything inside of you that you need to succeed. Everything. You have the power. You always did. Now go unleash it.

To You Creating Magic,

Jill

Meet the Author

Jill Christensen is one of the most in-demand and highest-rated female keynote speakers in the world today. Named a Top 200 Global Thought Leader to Watch and Top 101 Employee Engagement Influencer, she takes audiences on a journey that educates and inspires people to act. In the past four years, Jill has presented her proven strategy to re-engage employees to hundreds of thousands of people in 33 industries, 38 U.S. states, and 10 countries.

A former Fortune 500 Corporate Communications business executive with a Six Sigma Green Belt, Jill understands how organizations operate, and what they need to do differently to attract, retain, and engage both on-site and virtual employees. This makes her a valuable asset to any organization that wants to increase productivity, retention, customer satisfaction, and profitable revenue growth, and beat the competition.

Her first book, *If Not You, Who? How to Crack the Code of Employee Disengagement*, is a global best-seller, and her popular weekly blog was named a Top 100 Corporate Blog alongside of Apple and Microsoft. These resources are being used by small and midsize businesses, Fortune 500 firms, start-ups, government agencies, non-profits, and family-owned businesses in virtually every industry around the globe.

Thanks to Jill's passion, in-depth knowledge, energy, and ability to inspire, her keynote speech garners accolades from audience members and event planners such as: "Brilliant," "The Best Speaker I've Ever Heard," "Jill Has a Gift," and "Simply Outstanding."

Jill grew up in multiple U.S. states, attended college in Upstate New York, and resides in Denver, Colorado, with her two Maine Coon cats. She moved west from New Jersey due to her pioneering spirit, and love of the great outdoors, skiing, U.S. football, and live music.

A dual U.S./U.K. citizen, Jill's vision is to retire in multiple countries, and explore the world's diverse cultures, cuisines, natural habitats, and awe-inspiring historical sites.

But for now, Jill is still working on achieving her goal: to help fix every dysfunctional workplace in the world. To connect with Jill direct, and share your needs, thoughts, hopes, dreams, wishes, obstacles, and success stories, please reach out as follows:

Jill Christensen International, LLC
https://jillchristensenintl.com
jill@jillchristensenintl.com
+1.303.999.9224

To subscribe to Jill's complimentary award-winning blog (a five-minute weekly read):

- In the U.S., text the word **JILL** to the number **44144**
- Outside of the U.S., visit *https://bit.ly/pleasecountmein*

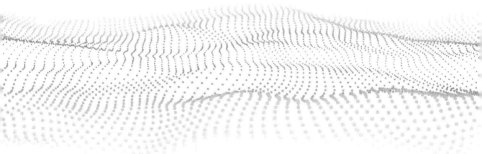